Apologetics Press is dedicated to the defense of New Testament Christianity. For over 35 years, we have provided faith-building materials for adults. We also have produced numerous materials for young people of all ages.

The Apologetics Press Early Reader Series is a set of books aimed at children in kindergarten through second grade. Depending on the age of your children, this series is flexible enough to allow parents to read to their children, read along with their children, or listen while their children read aloud to them.

The books in this series are filled with beautiful, full-color pictures and wonderful information about God, His creation, and His Word. These books are written on a level that early readers will enjoy, while drawing them closer to their Creator.

We hope you enjoy using the Apologetics Press Early Reader Series to encourage your children to read, while at the same time helping them learn about God and His creation.

See also our Learn to Read Series for 3- to 6-year-olds and our Advanced Reader Series for 2nd-3rd graders.
ApologeticsPress.org
(800) 234-8558

God Made Hair

by Jeff Miller, Ph.D.

Layout and Design by Tommy Hatfield

Copyright © 2018
Apologetics Press

All rights reserved. No part of this book may be reproduced in any manner whatsoever without written permission from the publisher.

ISBN-13: 978-1-60063-120-7

Library of Congress: 2018938874

Printed in China

God Made Hair

by Jeff Miller, Ph.D.

One of the useful and pretty
things God made was hair.
The Earth is full of hair!

Some insects have body parts that are like hair called seta (SEE-da).

Many plants and algae have body parts like hair, too. When we think of hair, we usually do not think about insects or plants.

We also might not think of flying, hairy creatures like bats.

Nor would we think about swimming creatures with hair, like whales or baby dolphins.

When we think about hair, we usually think about land mammals.

All mammals have hair. The hair on animal mammals is called fur.

Humans are not animals, but we are mammals. So we have hair. Hair grows everywhere you have skin, except for a few places, like your palms, the soles of your feet, your lips, the back of your ears, and your belly button.

Mammal hair has pigment in it that gives it color. Hair makes creatures look beautiful and fun to look at.

Human hair is the same color from its root to its tip.

Animal hairs, however, may change color along a single strand.

Fur can also protect creatures from harm by giving them cushion. Many animals have fur that helps to keep them warm.

Many evolutionists believe that human hair is not useful and is proof of evolution. That is not true.

Hair **is** useful.
It adds beauty to our bodies
and helps us stay warm.

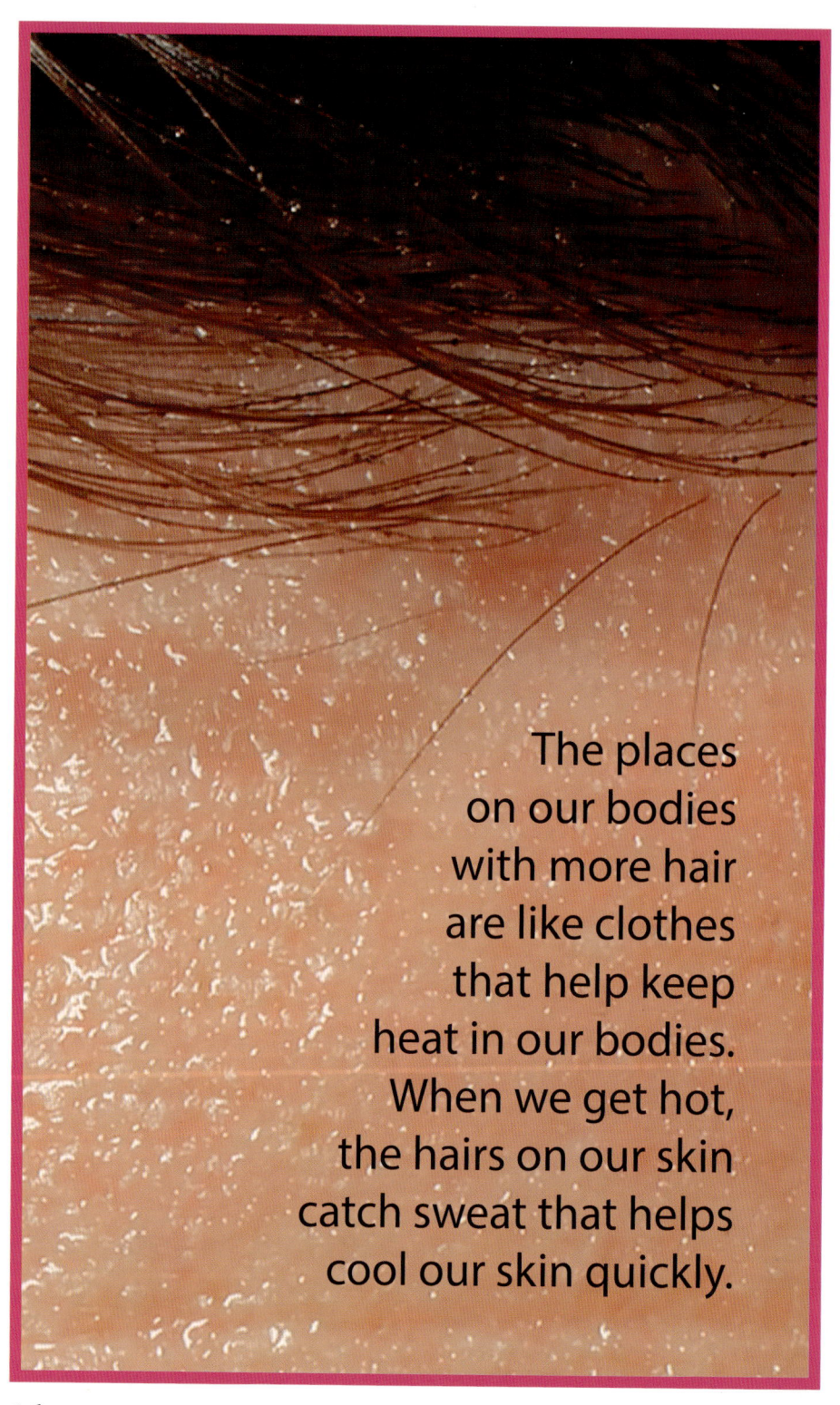

The places
on our bodies
with more hair
are like clothes
that help keep
heat in our bodies.
When we get hot,
the hairs on our skin
catch sweat that helps
cool our skin quickly.

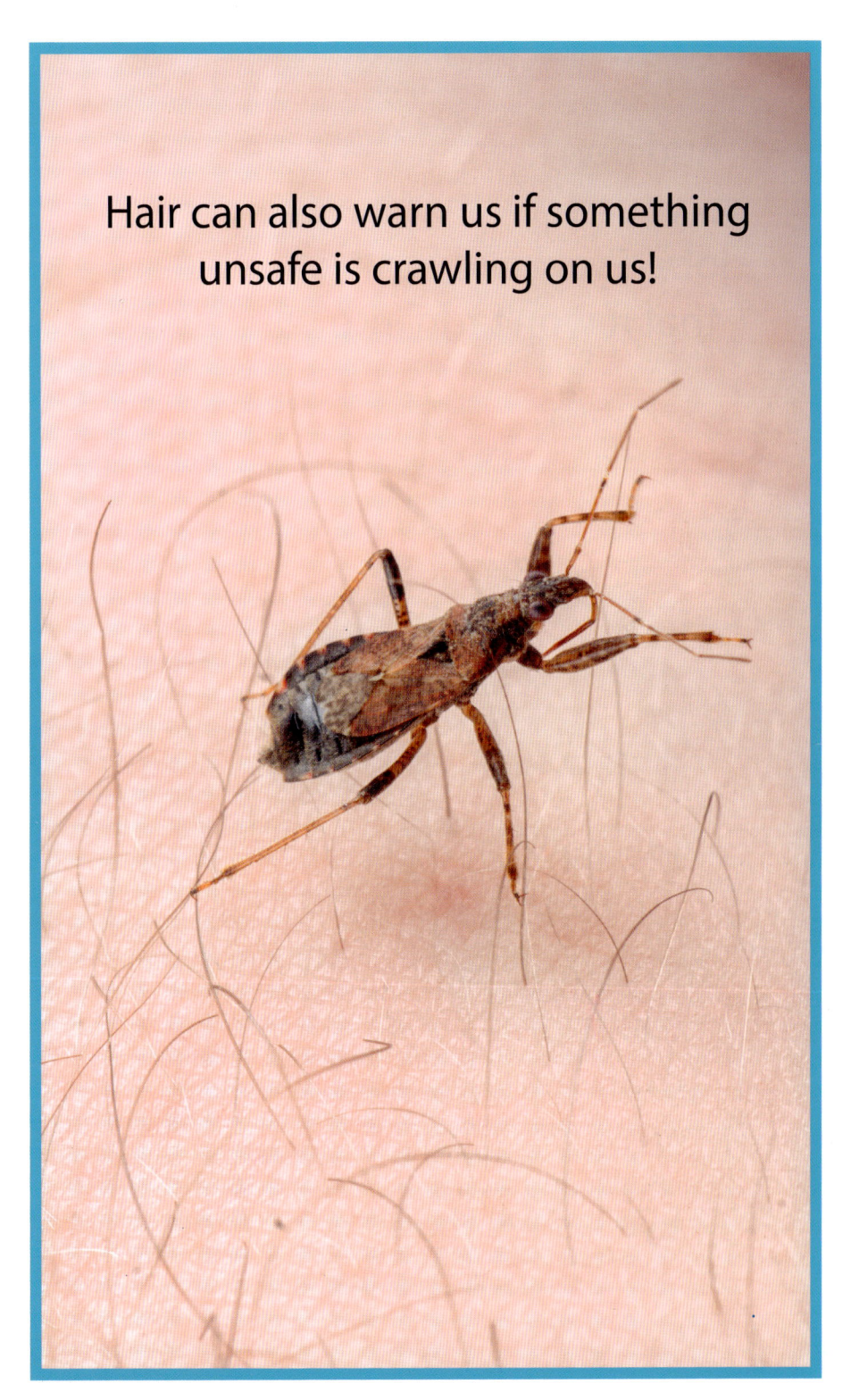

Hair can also warn us if something unsafe is crawling on us!

There are about five million hairs on the human body. We don't have as many hairs on our bodies as some animals. Some dogs have more hairs on their tiny bodies than do adult humans.

Evolutionists call humans "naked apes." We may have fewer hairs than many creatures, but we do have as many hairs on our bodies as chimps. Most of our hair is just shorter.

Humans stand up straight.
That means that our heads need
more protection from the Sun.
Thankfully, God made sure humans
tend to have longer hair on our
heads (where we need it).

Animal body hair is usually longer than most hair on human bodies. For most mammals, at a certain length, it falls out and is replaced with new strands.

The human **head**, however, can have as many as 150,000 hairs that can grow to be three feet long in six years—much longer than animal fur grows.

Our hair grows one-half of an inch every month. If you add up **all** of the hair growth on your head, that would be over 600 miles of hair in your life!

Mammal hairs are made of keratin (CARE-uh-tin).

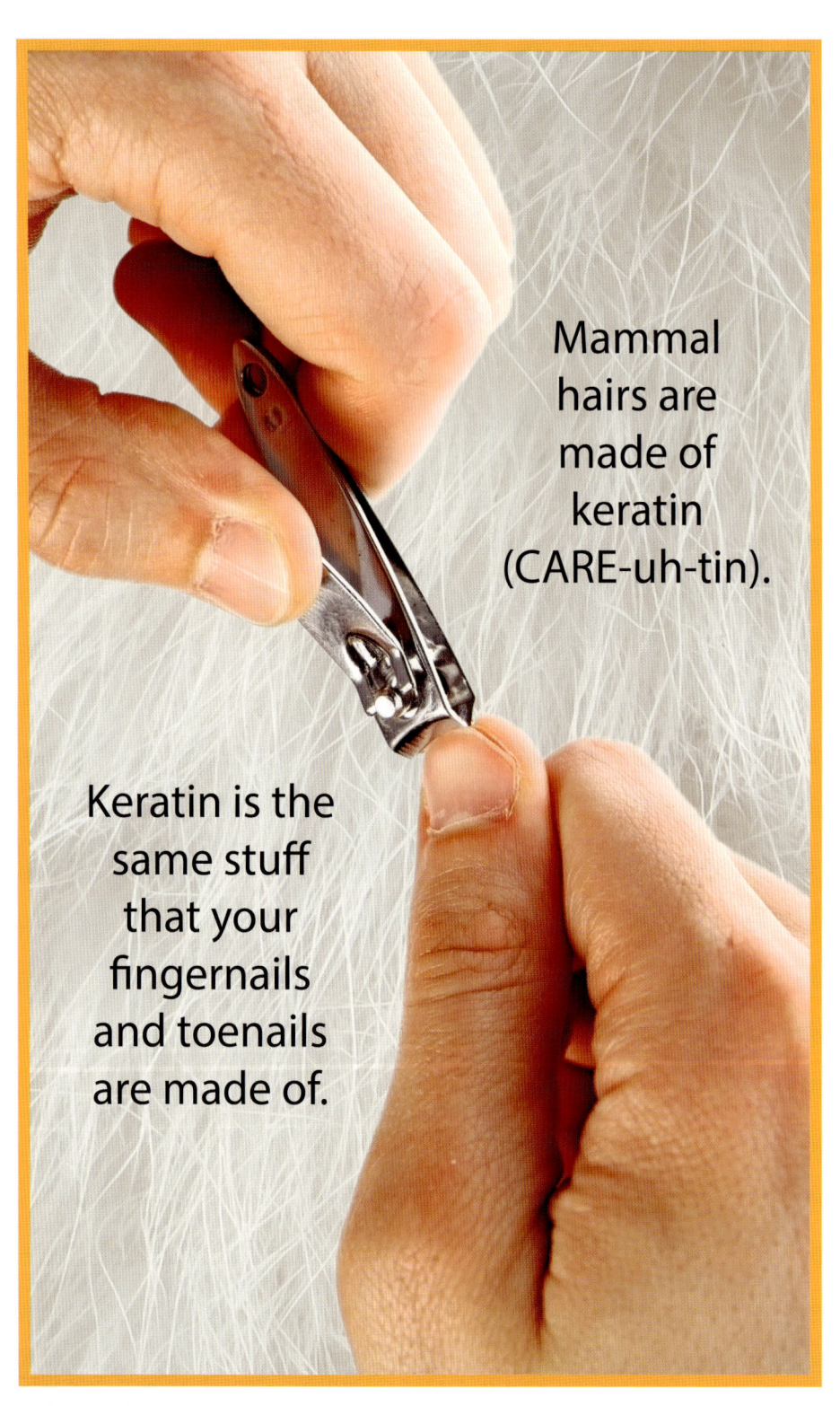

Keratin is the same stuff that your fingernails and toenails are made of.

Porcupine quills, cat whiskers, and sheep wool are also made of keratin.

Keratin is very strong.
So hair is very strong.
A single strand of hair
could hold an apple.

If you combine all of the hairs of your head, they could hold two elephants!

It takes a long time for hair to decay.

The oldest human hair ever found is well over 4,000 years old (before Abraham lived).

Hair is mentioned in the Bible about 100 times.

Have you read the story of Samson?

God created hair on days three, five, and six of Creation, and we should be thankful for it!